THRIVING TOGETHER:

5 SECRETS TO MINISTRY TEAM SUCCESS

James P. McGarvey, Ph.D.

TABLE OF CONTENTS

FOREWORD

If this is your first time finding one of our resources, welcome! Thank you for your dedication to serving your church and community through the ministry team of your place of worship. Thank you for spending the time to research, train, and sow into the lives of those that you serve with, for the protection and safety of God's people and the community. If we can be of assistance to you in the future, please visit our website at ChurchSafetyGuys.com and don't be afraid to reach out. We have many resources there and regularly travel across the United States to train and coach churches and houses of worship.

On The Journey Together,

James & Mike

Physical training is good, but training for godliness is much better, promising benefits in this life and in the life to come.

———

1 TIMOTHY 4:8

WHY THIS BOOK?

Whether you oversee a ministry team focused on church safety and security or another ministry-based team in your church or place of worship, everyone has one basic question when they're in leadership. "Am I doing this correctly?". It is easy to make assumptions that you are doing things the correct way, without having any structure, guidelines, or road map to determine what could potentially be the most correct way. After over 30 years in management, supervision, and leadership - both in public and private sectors, along with church and ministry-based organization, I'm happy to construct this roadmap for you to help you and make your team more successful at accomplishing their goals.

Your team cannot accomplish their goals without you. You regularly push them to accomplish goals that impact and direct the overall success of the team. Whether you are in the public/private sector or volunteering for a ministry/place of worship, volunteers will look to you for guidance, support and strength to be successful themselves. So how do you motivate, engage and connect with individuals that are volunteering in your church to effectively accomplish the results that you need to be successful in the community? Is that a mere fantasy or is it even really possible? The answer is yes. It is possible and it is not a fantasy. But it requires focused hard work. Hard work on the part of you, the leader, to go above and beyond. Above and beyond what you might ask? Above and beyond the normal procedural functions to accomplish whatever task that you are purposed to accomplish.

You see, when we first learn how to handle life, we regularly build constructs to be successful. Secretly inside, we all want a simple step by step process to be successful at whatever task we are trying to accomplish. If we can accomplish it by ourselves, the better we feel. If we have to reach out to others to accomplish the task, that makes us concerned, confused and vulnerable. You see, being vulnerable is an uncomfortable place to be. But the truth is, if we are relying on others to help us accomplish a task, we will be vulnerable. We cannot always control the variables around us. Especially in a church or ministry setting when we are relying on individuals that are only running on passion to successfully accomplish tasks. Being vulnerable means that we have the obligation to make our team of volunteers better with the skills that they have. If we can connect with them and somehow instruct, connect and engage with them, then everything will be ok. Maybe.

The truth is that our world is ever changing, along with the different generations of individuals that interact with it. While we can be consistent with the goals that we want to

> **~ In an ever-changing world, how do we engage? ~**

accomplish, we cannot always be consistent with the volunteers or individuals that we have because every person is different. Not only is every person different, but what engages, motivates and connects with people is different. Unfortunately, we cannot apply a "one size fits all" mentality when it comes to being successful with our ministry teams. We don't have the perfect answer to fix all of the potential problems that we have while we are leading a team at church (or any other place). The one source that is accurate and can provide the ultimate example and aid us in being an example is the Word of God. Within the Word of God, there is no better example of someone leading a diverse group of individuals, than Jesus Christ. Jesus exemplified the ultimate example of Servant Leadership and accomplished the task that He was given, by following five simple steps to guide His team of individuals (the Disciples).

If you are stuck in a rut of not being successful with a team at your church, then this book is for you. If you are trying to enhance your understanding of how people can be motivated, engaged or connected with, then this book is for you. If you are simply trying to understand how to implement a winning strategy to accomplish amazing things with your team, then this book is for you. Very infrequently do we get "do-overs" in life. But we do get the opportunity to move forward with a clean slate. Just as Jesus was forgiving and gracious with those that He led (the Disciples), God is gracious to us, demonstrating forgiveness and compassion when we need it the most. The practical application of this book is geared towards church safety and security ministries within the church or place of worship community. The Biblical principles, of it however, can be applied to any ministry team and used by any ministry leader to be successful.

Following the five steps in this book are not the end-all, cure all solution to life. Being successful with a team takes time and energy to effectively implement. If you miss a step, keep going. Try again. Be gracious and understanding with yourself, but be persistent. The volunteers that you are guiding want transparency, grace and understanding. You don't have to be a perfect leader. But you do need to be an honest individual that tries their hardest to effectively accomplish the goals of your team. Because if you are, that will be visible, regardless of anything else. The individuals that are volunteering will see your discipline to be successful and open and honest and support your efforts. Seeing a leader actively trying to be part of what they are working on with others, is very motivating and engaging. Spend the time working through this book and in deep consideration over the fiver principles expressed. Take time to apply them to your own leadership style and build into yourself to be a better leader. You have the ability to lead a phenomenal team in your church. You have been placed in this position, that you are in, for a reason. Be energized by the confidence and wisdom that only God can give, and work on being better. It will benefit you and those volunteering with you in the long purpose of serving in the church. It will make you a better person, and it will drive the success of your team.

This book is a combination of items that will help you lead as a better leader and give you the wisdom and insight to be successful not only at accomplishing your team's goals, but at being a better person and connecting with those that you serve with. Connecting with individuals not only benefits you personally, with the relationship aspects, but it also allows you to be more successful as a leader accomplishing your goals. What are the goals? Well, if you are serving in your church or place of worship, most likely you are working with a group of volunteers to make something happen. If you are serving in the capacity of safety and security you are leading a group of people to respond to (and mitigate) emergency situations as they happen within the church. What is success? Success cannot be defined with one attribute. It is a collection of events or attributes that brings everything together to fulfill the goals. Those goals might be simple and they might be more detailed. A team can have several different goals. It is a goal to operate procedurally, and it is a goal to support the mission of the church. It is important as you go through this book to remember that focusing on the content is practical to do both. My hope is that you can be successful and meet the operational goals as well as the goals of contributing stability to the mission of your church or place of worship.

Defining Concepts

As we go through the book there are two phrases that we will use regularly to convey thoughts and considerations for being successful with your team. These two phrases are concepts that we have regularly used and discussed in previous books, as well as on our podcast. They capture the essence of what many have learned and even few have successfully applied. We are defining them here so that you have a clear understanding when we use them throughout this resource.

1.) Relational Equity: Relational equity is the concept of building attributes that are beneficial to leading and directing individuals as a team. As you lead, and interact with the volunteers and individuals you come in contact with, you present yourself in an open and transparent way accomplishing what you need to, and building trust in your actions and presence with others. Not only does your actions, attitude and personal characteristics build trust

> ~As a leader, transparency is critical ~

with those that you are serving with, but they also build trust with those that you answer to in church or ministry leadership. As you accomplish tasks that are directed towards the goals of the ministry and the church or place of worship, that builds equity (or value) with everyone in an upward or downward direction on the line of people that you serve with. Your attitude plays a significant role in building that value with those above you, and as you work with other ministry leaders or those leading the church, their level of trust with your actions in handling emergency situations increase and solidify your relationship. As this continues, the individuals in authority above you, recognize that you can effectively handle emergency situations and they start developing additional levels of trust in your actions and in your operating logic. As you work with those that are volunteering or directly leading, you have the opportunity to do the same with them, building a culture of engagement and connectivity to them, because they understand your logic and chose to trust your direction based on past experience. In the ideal situation, after a period of time both the upper levels of ministry leadership (oversight) and those that you are serving with or directing, should both have significant levels of trust in your logic, problem solving, and operational capabilities because you have built transparency, openness, and trust to accomplish various tasks effectively and efficiently. If you find yourself in a place where you are leading a safety or security team and you don't feel as though you have "enough" experience to do that successfully, keep in mind that even the most experience individual in public safety has to demonstrate knowledge, problem solving skills, and logic with those around him that do not have

~ **Relational equity is confidence.** ~

trust in his skills because they do not know him (relational equity). As you respond to various incidents and attempt to handling things logically and to the best of your ability, remember that you are building trust with everyone around you, regardless of how large or small the incident is. There is always someone watching your actions and taking in how effectively you handled each and every situation. The more time that you spend developing your skills to be successful in the operational considerations, the more trust you have with those around you in your ability to make the right choice. As you build that trust, you can take advantage of using it to accomplish procedural actions (or goals) that you may not have had the ability to previously.

For example: I'm new to the team that I'm overseeing with my church safety team. I know that we need a decent first aid kit or trauma bag to respond to medical emergencies. The challenge is that I don't know how to use everything and my knowledge is limited. The best way to increase my knowledge is to take a class to learn more on emergency medicine and response. Taking a class in that information and then advising those around me, that I'm taking the class, builds trust and understanding. All of a sudden, those around me that are volunteering with me (or that I'm leading) and those in church leadership, have seen that I'm dedicated and passionate enough about this team and serving, that I'm willing to go take a class to be more effective and have more knowledge. That is building relational equity. People understand and learn to trust me more, because I have invested the time into learning concepts to be more effective and lead them in a better way. When I'm done taking the class, I will take the opportunity to meet with the church leaders (during the week) and outline what I've learned. That would build my relationship with them, along with showing them that I invested the time in learning new things. I will then mention to them, that in order to be successful with my new skill set and put it to use at the church or place of worship effectively, I need new equipment to do the job better. The opportunity is great because I can demonstrate that I know how to use the new equipment and it won't be wasted. Then I can train others that serve with me on the new equipment. In the end, the result is that I've built additional trust in the people I'm serving with, the people that oversee my safety and security ministry, and those that attend the church. Those that attend the church reap the benefits, because when my team and I respond to emergency situations to help them, they see that we are effectively trained on using new equipment. All of a sudden, our small team that originally didn't have equipment or know how to use it well, now has brand new equipment, is trained, and has the respect of other church members because the team can respond professionally. In turn, all of this together builds

> ~ Relational equity is credibility. ~

additional levels of trust with every category, solidifying the culture and perception of those around the team that we are an effective, trustworthy team. This is a long example, but hopefully you can see the importance of relational equity and how it works. The reality is that as long as you continually try to build into others and the perception of others, you will also build trust and you can use that trust to further the goals of the safety or security team.

All of this builds into the culture of your team and church, and gives you credibility with those that you are leading as well as those that you answer to. As you lead those on your ministry team, keep in mind that the more trust you have, the more engaged people volunteering will be, and the more successful you will be. That is why we bring up the concept of relational equity. As those volunteering on your team develops more trust in your actions and your leadership skills, you have the ability to engage and connect with them in ways that you might never have considered. In turn, because you were able to connect with them, the volunteers and individuals serving will have a better understanding of the goals of the team, and be more willing to give up their time when needed to contribute to the well-being of the ministry. When a volunteer connects to their leader and they adequately understand the goals of the team, they have a vested interest in the success of the ministry team and are more willing to assist when needed or necessary.

2.) Mission of the Church: When we talk about the "mission" of the church, what exactly do we mean? Webster defines "mission" as being "A specific task with which a group or person is charged". The fact is that every church or place of worship is going to have a different task or mission that they feel is vital to the community that they are in. One of the churches that I recently attended had the mission of "Worship, Grow, Serve & Go". They are encouraging individuals from the community to come in, worship together, grow in knowledge and relationships, serve the community together and go impact others for Jesus Christ. If that is their purpose and mission parameters for the community, then every ministry team within the church needs to be aware and supportive of that purpose and mission. If

~What is the Mission of Your Place of Worship? ~

they are not aware and supportive, then ministry teams will get sidetracked and could potentially do more damage than good reaching that goal in the community. Every ministry team leader needs to drive their team to focus on that mission, because at the end of the day, those are the goals that the church or place of worship intends to contribute to the community. Safety and security play an intricate role within the ministry teams in the church. They are the one ministry team that directly impacts the operational procedures of each team focusing on the overall mission of the church. When the other teams are trying to accomplish their goals supportive of the church mission, the safety and security team is the ministry team that keeps things moving smoothly by mitigating the unexpected that occurs.

Every place of worship can have a different mission. If I took the time to evaluate or google any church in my community, each one would have a different focus. That's not unusual or wrong, but it means that every organization (place of worship) is going to have a different focus when it comes to how their ministry teams support their actions. A volunteer cannot just go from attending one church to another, without first analyzing how the church's mission has changed and what new adjustments they need to personal make with their interaction in the church ministry teams. Every church has a place in supporting communities. Thus, understanding how safety or security teams interact with different ministries and can impact them in a positive way to assist with accomplishing the church mission takes time and careful consideration. Not every safety or security team is created equal, and not every team functions in the same way. The teams that I have seen that are successful, spend an enormous amount of time focusing on running with similarities to public safety enterprises. They gracefully

> **~ Be supportive of the overall purpose of the church. ~**

interject themselves into events, projects and various committees to ensure that everything is carefully considered when things take place within the church. The key is being supportive of the overall purpose. When church safety and security teams are supportive of the mission of the church, everything runs much more smoothly, because everything that could possibly go wrong has a plan and is covered. When church safety and security teams simply do one function- and that's to act as a security guard, it's not building into the operational procedures of the other ministry teams or supporting them. Every ministry has a purpose to support the goals and mission of the church. As the safety and security team contribute their time and energy into ensuring everything runs smoothly and no emergencies take place that are unmitigated, the church and other ministry teams can focus on their specialty. When we start treating safety and security as an integral part of church and place of worship operations, along with the concept of engaging with others as Jesus did, big things *will* happen!

3.) Perception is reality: It's been said that what is "seen" as actually happening, is not always what exactly is happening. When the discussion is made regarding perception, there are two classifications within the church. First, the perception of the leadership on the church operations and continuity of accomplishing their mission. Second, the perception of accomplishing this mission from the attendees (or members) point of view. While this has an enormous role in the stability of the culture, often times, from our experience, there is a significant disconnect between what the church leadership sees and the attendees see. The challenge with this is for the two perspectives to interact and come close together, building a culture where attendees are content with what is happening, and leadership has the support of the members. It is important to remember that while policies and procedures may change, as leaders, our focus should be on taking the necessary steps to ensure that the culture of the church is in fact where it needs to be, according to the benefit of all ministries operating. If the congregants feel that the environment is safe and secure and that is a focus of the leadership, then the church will be successful because the attendees are more engaged. If the attendees are more engaged, then they will feel as though they have more value through the activities of the church and be more involved. Unfortunately, "feelings" do not always line up with the culture and operations of what is really happening. This is why it is mindful to consider perception, because often times there can be a significant disconnect between leadership and what is truly happening within the church.

LET US NOT BECOME WEARY IN DOING

GOOD, FOR AT THE PROPER TIME WE

WILL REAP A HARVEST IF WE

DO NOT GIVE UP

GALATIANS 6:9

Chapter 1

QUALITY
OVER QUANTITY

In the fast paced and high-tech world that we are in, it's challenging not to bring that mentality into church and allow it to find a home. Being a leader over a ministry requires that we think outside the box, and regularly evaluate policies and procedures to accomplish our tasks and goals. There is a great deal to be said for the period of time when we did not have all of those influences, within the church. From a leadership perspective, we are pushed and pushed (since youth) that the faster

~ **The volunteer needs to feel meaningful engagement.** ~

and better we can accomplish tasks and goals the more accomplished we are. The reality is that as generations have changed, we have the opportunity to connect with those that are around us with meaningful engagement. As we lead those around us that volunteer with us, and motivate them to continue serving, we have to connect with them so they are driven to seek their own success through the accomplishments. As we mentioned in the book "Inspire, Influence, Impact", the generation of the individual plays a tremendous role in determining how to connect with the person that is volunteering. Our culture today is driven to be successful, but there needs to be a tangible benefit to the volunteers. If an individual is interested in volunteering, they desire a personal connection first, and then once that is established, they are encouraged and connect to the leader, and want to spend more time with the leader supporting the activity. They need to believe in the leader that the leader is in fact wanting to spend time with them and connect with them, above and beyond the task at hand that needs to be accomplished. If the task is a ministry team at a church or place of worship, they want to see the benefit for themselves personally, in spending the time serving. Serving the community, serving the church and serving others should be a motivating action, but it has to be obvious.

~ The benefits of serving have to be obvious. ~

It isn't enough anymore to simply meet someone and ask them to help or volunteer. The volunteer needs to see and feel an emotional engagement or connection with the person asking; in many cases before they ask. If the connection is not there, then individuals will be less likely to actually give their time to the activities of the ministry team at church. The volunteers need to have their emotional needs met through serving. Gone are the days where individuals were compelled to attend church and volunteer for ministry teams simply because "it was the right thing to do". That certainly could be directed to a different and older, more mature generation.

When we train volunteers to serve and invest their time, we don't want to fail. No one wants to waste their time by investing it into a ministry that isn't successful. When we invest our time into teaching others how to accomplish tasks, to meet the ministry goals, we need to make sure that we are doing so at a pace they can adequately comprehend. If you have been asked to be the leader of a ministry such as church safety or security, there is a chance that you are well experienced in that subject. The individuals that are volunteering may not be, and as the leader you need to make sure that you are spending sufficient amount of time teaching them in a way that they can be most successful. Successfully understanding training and being able to accomplish ministry team functions is a motivation in and of itself. Everyone wants to be successful and have purpose. Helping someone see that purpose through a church ministry team is invigorating and one of the roles and responsibilities of the ministry leader.

As a leader you should be able to:

- Adequately articulate the mission and purpose of the church.

- Describe and articulate the goals of the team.

- Train volunteers to effectively accomplish the goals of the team through various tasks.

- Be solid in procedures, policies, and convictions, but also be graceful to new ideas and discussion from volunteers.

- Seek to connect and engage with volunteers beyond just their volunteer times.

- Be able to read the culture of the team to adjust the outlook when necessary.

- Understand the needs of the volunteer and their motivation based on their age, demographic, and generation.

How to connect and engage:

- Spend time getting to know volunteers and their personalities outside of church.

- Understand that everyone has a different motivational factor based on who they are.

- Regular engagement on the ministry team, with other volunteers can build unity.

- Spend time in prayer and Bible study.

- Grab coffee or lunch someday, during the week.

- Pick a mutual entertaining sport - like fishing or shooting to do together to get to know each other better.

When we apply the idea of quality over quantity with ministry teams, let's use the example of church safety and security. The safety or security team typically falls under the oversight structure of hospitality or first impressions within the operational procedures of the church. While it is important to ensure that procedures and policies are followed, it is just as important to be gracious and demonstrate grace to those attending the church or those that we come in contact with (2 Corinthians 9:8). How you treat people (especially those volunteering) can make all the difference in the world! It can make a difference in their personal life (for volunteering) and it can make an amazing difference in accomplishing the goals of the ministry team. Instead of always critiquing make sure to coach and encourage as well. Individuals that are volunteering want to know that what they are doing has value as well as filling their own need for engagement.

Quick Tips for the Leader:

- Encourage those volunteering with positive reinforcement.

- If you have to coach or correct/critique someone, make sure to do it in an open environment- privately so as not to create a scene (unless it is a topic that needs to be addressed with the entire team).

- Distinguish what is important to critique and what is not. Not following a church mandated policy or procedure is important. Someone being on their phone is less important.

- Not every mistake that is made by volunteers needs to be called out.

- Be transparent with your volunteers. If you don't know the answer to a question, tell them the truth, but also spend the time to get the appropriate answer and direction, whether it is from the church leadership or somewhere else.

Quality over quantity also implies that as a leader you will guide the volunteers through the fog of understanding what is important compared to what is not (or something of lesser importance). When you are directing them, remember that they may not have the experience or knowledge that you do. It is vital to be able to determine things that are extremely important (and "a hill worth dying on") and things that can be overlooked or possibly re-addressed at a later time. Not every problem that needs to be solved, is an emergency. Prioritize and plan out an outline of the day that you are serving and how you would like it to go. Being intentional will allow you to ensure that you are accomplishing the daily procedural tasks that you need to. The concept of quality over quantity aids to the establishment of relational equity with the team volunteers and the church leadership overseeing your ministry team.

> ~ Leaders guide volunteers through the fog of priorities. ~

Quick Tips for the Volunteer:

- When the team leader asks you to do something realize that it may be coming directly from the oversight pastor or leadership structure and not directly him.

- Sometimes the leader directing the ministry needs you to listen and complete a task without questioning it.

- The ministry team leader often times sees more globally with team operations than volunteers do.

- Be flexible that you might not always understand what you're asked to do, but it might fight into the bigger picture of operations for the church or place of worship.

- Seek to understand, but listen to learn.

- Be honest and open with your team leader. They appreciate your truthfulness.

- Be passionate about doing things the right way and be thorough.

- You are being depended on to make things happen. Be dependable. It means a lot.

Whether you are taking over a ministry team or trying to build a new one, it should be a slow process. The initial assembly of the team may happen quickly, but encouraging the mix of gaining credibility is a long-term goal. Consistency is critical in obtaining credibility and relational equity. As a leader it is important to emphasize that volunteers be consistent to ensure that the processes and procedures

> **~ Perception of non-volunteers or church members must be considered. ~**

are consistent. Being consistent offers reassurance to those attending the church or place of worship that you and your team will be there to accomplish tasks and secure the goal. For the example, it is not unreasonable to expect a year or two for the ministry team to be set up and running in a solid functional way. Much of the church perception on the effectiveness of the team (whether it is true or not) comes to consistency and quality. This being a key factor, it's important to remember that as a leader it is your responsibility to also have the volunteer and ministry team's back (supporting them both adequately). This means that as a leader you are also responsible for public relations and ensuring that individuals throughout the church or place of worship understand what you truly do. From gently explaining to others the operation functions of your team, to being visible and helping out, any action that you take to display commonality between your team and other teams or functions in the church go a long way in providing a stable culture. Stable cultures always foster quality and are the foundational characteristic for a successful ministry team.

COMMIT

YOUR WORK TO THE LORD,

AND YOUR PLANS WILL BE

ESTABLISHED.

Chapter 2

LEAD WITH ENGAGEMENT AND MEET PEOPLE WHERE THEY ARE

One of the most effective ways to engage with others that are on the same ministry team, is to be relatable. Sometimes being relatable simple means being a good listener and empathetic. Meeting people where they are is realizing that we are all human and there are times when we fail. No one is perfect and we have the perfect reminder of God's grace to extend to those that might have dashed our hopes or expectations. When serving with a volunteer, it's easy to get pulled into an individuals' personal drama and be critical. The key to success for a leader is to overlook the drama and push forward to accomplishing tasks and goals. Everyone has a different background and story. Regardless of the volunteer's story, they are there to serve, and when they are struggling with something in their life, they need the support and empathy of someone that is genuinely concerned about their well-being. They need that more than an individual being

> ~ Volunteers need empathy and support to be successful. ~

judgmental over their actions or past actions. That doesn't remove the responsibility of any volunteer to serve in an honest manner with integrity and Biblical principles. What it does mean is that as leaders we need to be understanding that some times life events can spill over to the actions of a volunteer and impact their effectiveness, short term or long term. Short term can be overlooked in many cases. Long term prompts a sit-down discussion over how to remove some of the distractions to continue accomplishing the team mission and that of the church. In some cases, a leave of absence

> ~ Volunteers need consistency with those they are engaged with. ~

may be necessary for an individual that is struggling with balancing life outside of church and volunteering. Whatever is happening, or whichever course of actions is decided, keep in touch with that individual. Remember that they are serving and not generally getting compensated for serving. Just because they have removed themselves from immediate service, does not mean that they aren't interested in you staying connected and engaged with them. Quite the opposite. They are hoping and anticipating that you are consistent with the personal relationship and are motivated to help them and be a true friend. That is meeting someone where they are. Be a friend and engaged with the volunteer before their supervisory "boss" with ministry.

Probably one of the biggest aspects of engagement with others is being available to listen and interact in a positive way. Even if you don't completely agree with the individual or their viewpoint, take the opportunity to look beyond the immediate discussion or interaction. Understand that it's ok to not always agree with someone or have a differing opinion.

Quick Tips for Engagement:

- Be positive and affirming (to the person).

- Listen and be empathetic (even if you don't agree with them).

- Look for ways to unify and bond with the person doing things together outside of ministry.

- We are only as successful as those around us, supporting us.

- Be authentic, transparent and genuine.

- Be present for what is happening in the volunteer's life.

- Offer to pray with them and be supportive.

- When your team meets on a regular basis, pray before you start your normal tasks.

When it comes to engaging with people or meeting them where they are, Jesus was the perfect example of an individual that went above and beyond to invest in others. At least 40 times in the New Testament, Jesus interacted with people and either began the conversation or listened to others bring their situations to

~ Jesus regularly demonstrated empathy to those around Him. ~

him. During the times that He initiated the conversation, He made the point of also demonstrating listening skills, and being empathetic (John 4:7-42 - Woman at the Well). Even when He culturally should not have bothered, He made an effort to listen and invest in others to authentically help them with the challenges they were facing on a personal level. In other situations, people reached out to Him for guidance, and He never turned anyone away. Part of being engaged with others and motivating them, is giving back to them and meeting their needs, when they need it. As a leader, making yourself available to help others is critical to show relational equity to those who are volunteering with you. When you invest in making yourself available to others, it demonstrates that you care,

> ~ Go above and beyond with volunteers to ensure they are treated well. ~

above and beyond the task and mission at hand. Certainly, there are times, when discussions and conversations are better suited for scheduled times. In the middle of a Saturday and Sunday service is not the best time to be discussing personal situations. There have been times that I have stopped what I was doing, and stepped away to help others or talk to them, and encourage them because something was going on in their life that was impacting their focus. As you get to know volunteers better you are investing in their lives and developing your relationship with them to make it a mutually beneficial relationship above or beyond tasks and goals. The tasks and goals that you are able to accomplish are important, but ministry is about helping each other and supporting the mission of the church together. If you are treating everyone like a simple volunteer, they will not be volunteering long. At some point in time, the engagement and motivation that they need to feel valued will disappear and you will no longer have people to volunteer with. As long as I have served in ministry settings or on ministry teams, I have always appreciated when someone says "thank you" to me for giving up my time. I am not generally motivated by words of affirmation, but I enjoy people being grateful for me giving of my time and accomplishing something. There have certainly been many situations and occasions where I have not been thanked, and that's ok too. But keeping that in mind, one thing that I have always intentionally done, is to take the opportunity after (or during) the task to intentionally connect with individuals and thank them for volunteering of their time. Do I have to? Probably not. Is it something that connects to them and helps engage with them, motivating them to continue? Absolutely. Everyone likes knowing they are valued and contribute to the success and purpose of something. As a leader, that's where you can step in and be extremely effective. As you engage with others and meet them where they are, you are contributing to them and their purpose along with their value. Your interaction then becomes something that is mutually beneficial for both of you as you work towards accomplishing the mission of the church and fulfilling a volunteers needs.

GOD SENT HIS SON TO BE

THE *Savior* OF THE

WORLD.

1 JOHN 4:14

Chapter 3

FOLLOW JESUS' EXAMPLE OF WORKING SMARTER, NOT HARDER & CREATE DISCIPLES

When Jesus was on earth, He had a very specific mission to accomplish and tasks to perform to accomplish that mission. While He was focused on completing the tasks to the success of His mission and the obedience of His Father, He also made the time to stop and creatively help those along the way. He used His time to instruct those around Him, including the twelve Disciples, for the purpose of giving them value and purpose and to fulfill His commands and the prophecy of the Old Testament. All twelve individuals were from different backgrounds and had a different knowledge base. Jesus took the time to instruct them personally and help them understand

~ Jesus picked passionate people to serve in His mission. ~

concepts and principles, when someone else would have ignored them or chosen others to be around. Jesus picked people that were passionate about doing the right thing and being honest and transparent, along with authentic.

Culturally, there was nothing special about any of them. But the common thread that all of them experienced with their character was that they all wanted to serve Jesus because He gave them a value in themselves that they didn't even quite understand. Not only did He give them a value, but He took time to be intentional and ensure that they were challenged to be better and more productive people. Being more productive and realizing their value in Christ, they changed the world for Him, sharing the Gospel and starting the first church. By connecting with them, He gave them a motivation that they didn't have previously. He met people where they were and took the initiative to reach out to those that He was with, as well as those along His journey. He left room in His schedule to converse

> ~ Jesus made time in His schedule for interruptions from people. ~

with people that didn't feel like they met social norms to talk to someone as "good" and upstanding as He was. He challenged the status quo with encouraging others to love God first, others second, and create disciples - the three main commandments in the New Testament from Him. Jesus set the example for us to follow by being intentional, and following His directive to make disciples. As a ministry leader, it is your goal to create disciples as you accomplish tasks and procedural goals in supporting the mission of the church. If you don't have creating disciples as a goal in your ministry framework, you need to add it.

Creating a disciple isn't just the pastor's role or responsibility. As we pour into the lives of those that we engage with, within the ministries and functions of the church, it's important that all of us contribute to the process of discipling making, since Jesus left it as a directive.

Matthew 28:19-20 says:

> *"Therefore, go and make disciples of all nations, baptizing them in the name of the Father and of the Son and of the Holy Spirit, and teaching them to obey everything I have commanded you. And surely, I am with you always, to the very end of the age." (Matthew 28:19-20).*

Since it is all of our responsibilities, leaders play a critical role in every ministry, engaging and connecting with others to coach them and lead them in a knowledge of Jesus. Developing effective community within the church and helping the church fulfill its mission means that we need to establish a connection with others and be receptive to the needs of those around us that

~ Developing effective community within the church is important. ~

we are volunteering with. You might not have the opportunity to directly impact every volunteer in the church or place of worship, but you have the opportunity as a leader to impact the individuals that are volunteering with your ministry team. Engaging with others and building into their lives is an unbelievably rewarding endeavor. Not only does it help them, but it will help you. It helps you because it keeps you focused on what is important and valuable, and keeps your mind, spirit, and body sharp to successfully accomplish the goals of the ministry team. As you invest in the lives of others, God will use that action to bless you and your family, and reward your efforts. Sometimes that reward is relationships. Other times God rewards in different ways. But

> ~ God will use action to bless you and your family. ~

no matter how much you give- you can't outgive God. Beyond finances, when you give to others, God uses it and becomes the force multiplier to do amazing things.

Quick Tips for Working Smarter & Creating Disciples:

- Be innovative! Ask others their opinion on processes.

- Delegate on your team! Increase other's value and self- worth and spend time training them to effectively do tasks with or without your oversight. That helps them grow and takes things off your list to do.

- Be intentional and transparent.

- Learn as you go, but realize that people are looking to you for guidance, leadership and your attitude on topics. Their attitude will be your attitude.

- It's ok to make mistakes. Own up to it and change it.

- Establish a connection/engagement with others- make it a priority to reach out and connect with one volunteer (a different one) each week.

- Pray that God will use you to further His message and His service and that He would put you in the right place at the right time to help others.

THE SON OF MAN CAME NOT

TO BE SERVED BUT TO SERVE

OTHERS AND TO GIVE HIS LIFE

AS A RANSOM FOR MANY.

MATTHEW 20:28

Chapter 4

DEMONSTRATE EMPATHY

Famous author C.S. Lewis stated: "Hardships often prepare ordinary people for an extraordinary destiny". If you believe that God has a purpose and plan for each of our lives, then you have to acknowledge there are times in our life when we have ups and downs. As leaders, we need to demonstrate empathy towards those that are volunteering on our team. Empathy is the understanding of another's feelings in any particular situation. We don't have to approve of their feelings or agree with them. Leading a group of volunteers, if you invest into the lives of those serving, and you attempt to understand their feelings, you will be an extremely successful leader. I often have told the story of one of my favorite bosses when I

~ You don't have to agree with someone, but you do need to listen. ~

worked in retail management. Every day before I closed the store (I had the evening shift), my boss and I would walk to the store and talk about the things that needed to get done before we closed for the day. If we had extra time, we would talk about our families, and how they were doing and goals working with the company. One thing that always stuck with me, was that every day we would walk around the store any employee that he would see, he would intentionally stop and say hello to them by name, and ask them about one thing that he remembered. In some cases, it might have been a question about a relative, or another person it might have been a question on their child. No matter what the role of that individual was, my boss could have literally asked them to do anything for him. In fact, you could see their disposition light up every time he would ask them that one question. They were literally thrilled to have the opportunity to talk about themselves in that context, and they were even more thrilled that he actually remembered them.

> ~ Being transparent and genuine goes further than anything else. ~

Not only did they respect him, but after a few times of noticing his habits, I realized that he was genuine and transparent about being concerned about them. He was investing time and energy into each of them, in a way that would pay dividends, but would also make them better employees. From that point forward, I made it a special point to do the same. My employees and team members respected me for taking the time to engage and connect with them, that on many occasions when I had special projects or something serious to complete, they would volunteer, just because they knew that it would personally benefit me. I got into the habit of asking someone to perform a task by saying "Can I ask you a favor?". If they hesitated, I would follow it up with a quick "it would really help me out quite a bit". Then without a second thought, they would say "sure, what can I do?". People like to know that they are contributing to the value of a bigger picture. People like to know that themselves have value added to their lives and purpose. The employees would help me, and do what I asked, because they knew whatever I was asking of them, had value. I could have just told them to do the task without a second thought, and yes, they would've had to listen to me because I was the boss. But by connecting with them on a different level, it gave them an opportunity to help me, and it allowed me to work with them in a way that was more meaningful to them and to the company we worked for. Reading that illustration, some might think "Well, they were getting paid to do a job, they should have done it regardless of the interaction". The truth is that we all function and operate better, when we do so without be beat over the head with the "because" factor. The "because" factor is when we choose to do the right thing, *because* of getting compensated, not because of the different levels of value it adds to us or to those that we are helping. No one at church that volunteers, typically gets compensated for their time or energy in a physical way. People are compensated mentally and spiritually because they are helping others and the community and contributing to the purpose of the church. They truly do not "have to" do anything. They can leave at any time and ignore direction from a leader they do not like or agree with.

Not every situation might be as straightforward as that. But if you get into the habit of giving to those that are volunteering, and make the connection of being a personable leader, and emphasize working together with them to accomplish the goals, you will be successful in demonstrating empathy and it will connect with them on multiple levels. Jesus demonstrated empathy regularly with those that were around Him, even if He didn't agree with them. He understood where their logic was and took time to be personable with them. He could have commanded His twelve Disciples to accomplish tasks, and as their leader, they probably would have without a second thought. But, He didn't. He connected with each of them

> ~ Jesus spent time connecting and engaging with those around Him. ~

(even the one that betrayed Him), for their benefit. You see, being a leader means that not only are trying to accomplish tasks and goals supporting the mission of your church, but you need to contribute to the lives of those volunteering. If you don't think that you can adequately do that (with logic and reasoning) then leadership might not be the right position for you. I believe that every person has the potential to be a significant leader when given the right opportunity. Not everyone aspires to be a leader, but as a leader, it is critical to invest time into those that are volunteering within your ministry team.

Jesus demonstrated empathy for people around Him while He was doing His Earthly ministry. He could relate and empathize with people. If they were in need of direction (whether personal or spiritual) He was available to give them guidance and help them accordingly. Those around Him knew that He was an individual that would regularly demonstrate empathy towards those that He ministered to. He also demonstrated empathy towards those that were His closest friends. In John 11:30-35, Jesus's friend Lazarus died, and He used the situation to connect with people and demonstrate His empathy. In verse 35 of John Chapter 11, Jesus cried. This verse, the shortest verse in the Bible demonstrates so much transparency and truth. Jesus with all of His capability as fully God and fully Man, took the opportunity to spend time with those mourning and to be of one mind with them, but did not chide them for being foolish or for showing emotion. He demonstrated emotion and empathy towards them and connected with them. Sometimes demonstrating empathy as a leader is simply listening to the concerns of a volunteer or team member.

~ Be flexible to relate and empathize with people. ~

Another Bible passage that emphasizes the importance of empathy as being a Biblical concept is Romans 12: 15, which says: "Rejoice with those that rejoice, and weep with those that weep". We are wired to be protective and be concerned with our own wellbeing and the wellbeing of those around us with

~ What impacts one volunteer impacts the team. ~

the emphasize on our own needs. This ideology and concept would be similar to Maslow's Hierarchy of Needs. At times this can be detrimental, because we end up so focused on our own needs that we don't even see what is going on around us, or connect with others around us that are suffering to help them deal with their situations. The Apostle Paul references being one with others and demonstrating emotion when they do. At times that can be challenging because we have a desire to stay away from drama or the misfortune of others. In a ministry team, however, what impacts one volunteer impacts everyone, including the leader. The best way to build a relationship is to support those that are suffering and make the effort to understand what they are going through and offer to help. They may not accept your help, but they will appreciate the offer to be there for them when they need it. Ephesians 4:32 says "Be kind and compassionate to one another, forgiving one another, just as in Christ God forgave you." We are reminded that it is appropriate for us to demonstrate empathy towards others and be compassionate to them, because God, through Christ has demonstrated compassion and forgiveness to us.

Quick Tips for Demonstrating Empathy:

- Be sure to make direct eye contact when they are talking.

- Focus on being there in the moment- try to avoid using electronics or checking your phone.

- Give people your full attention and be genuinely curious about their life.

- Listen with a goal of understanding.

- Don't offer advice, unless it is asked for!

- Acknowledge their feelings.

- Ask how you can help.

- Occasionally when someone needs a distraction from something happening in their life, they will ask to volunteer more or be more heavily involved with the ministry team. It's ok to increase their involvement, but be careful not to overwhelm them.

- Engage and connect with them.

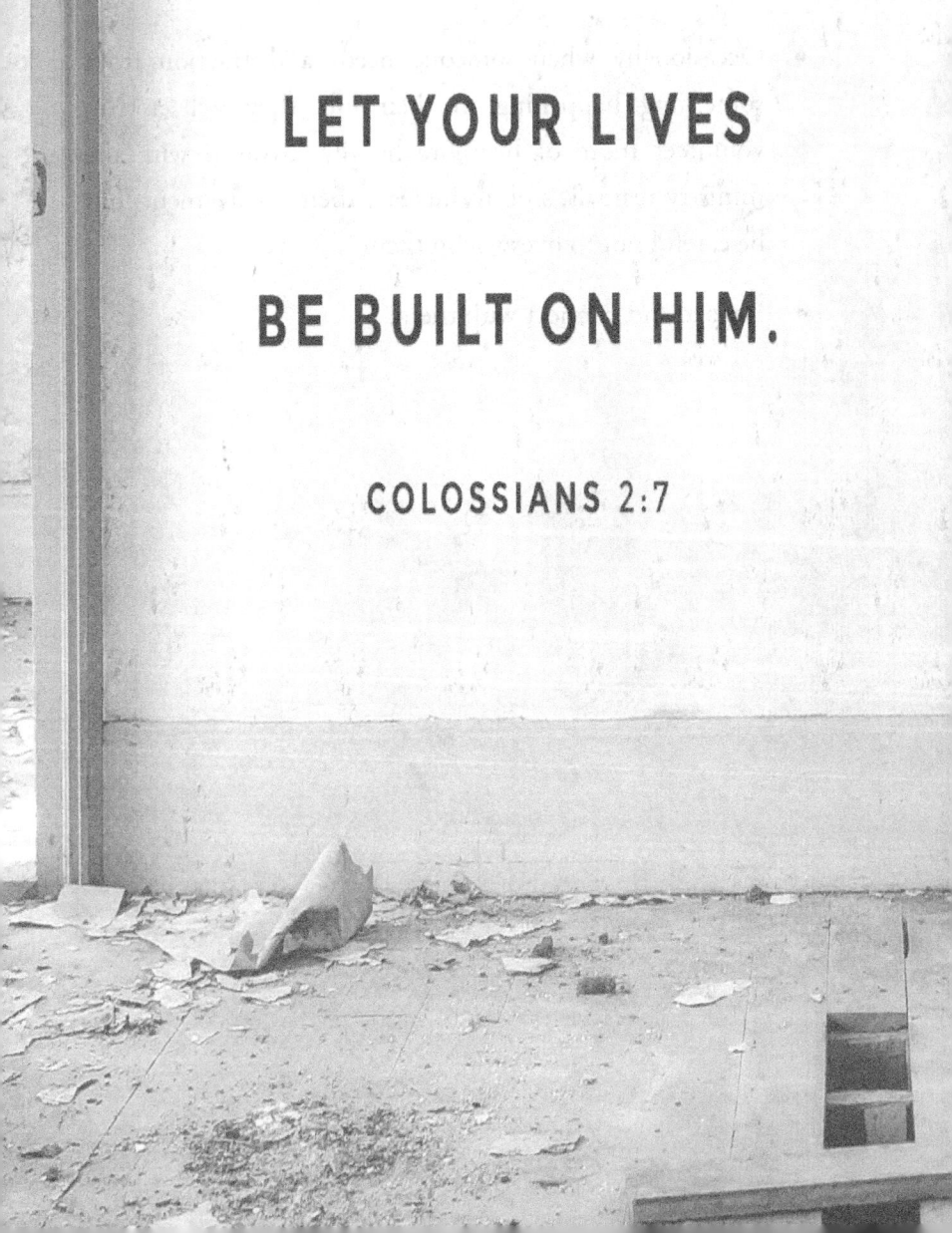

Chapter 5

EXEMPLIFY GRACE

Exemplifying grace is a key component to having success as a leader over a ministry team. As leaders, leadership development is a gradual progression. We grow as we learn to manage situations that directly or indirectly impact us. We all have the opportunity to become better leaders. In this case, the situations that happen to us can usually be evaluated and then successfully solved by the processes and procedures outlined by the church. Grace being the component that it is, encompasses the active actions of servant leadership and empathy.

> ~ Demonstrating grace can motivate and guide volunteers. ~

Grace is the application of leadership principles to accomplish more with understanding and flexibility. Leadership is being able to understanding the type of culture you want to develop with the help of the team. In this case, whether it is church safety and security or another ministry, understanding the culture and its focus is important. Demonstrating grace can help you motivate and guide those that are helping you accomplish that mission and the mission of the church. It allows you to be receptive to change, partner with others to accomplish tasks, provide a stable learning environment, offer a blame free environment, build team unity and it allows for a flexible, adaptive framework. The truth is that regardless of how we're leading or serving, we all want to be successful. The only way that is possible is to build grace into all of the aspects of leadership. It then has a "trickle down" effect on the people within the team and keeps them motivated and focused to do what needs to be accomplished. Not only does it allow volunteers to have more motivation and focus, but it adds more value to the team, when leadership is applied successfully. Everyone

> ~ Leaders are responsible for their own development. ~

wants to answer the question; "What's in it for me?". When we apply principles of grace to leadership strategies, we find that volunteers are happy, content, motivated, and engaged, performing better. It is your responsibility to develop your own leadership skills to be a more effective leader to your team. One of those ways to develop skills is to "always be training". Another way, is to do things that challenge you, based on your opportunities and strengths.

What leaders do:

1.) Understand the desired outcome.

2.) Understand the current reality.

3.) Understand how to get from the current reality to the desired outcome.

4.) Review and assess assets.

5.) Review and assess potential and real challenges.

Leaders have the responsibility of looking at the real challenges and potential challenges as well as the distractions from the mission of the team and ultimately the mission of the church. Recognizing distractions is important, because it can cause your team to miss its purpose. As you develop your skills to guide and lead those on your team, remember that everyone has a choice to be there. In many cases if you are volunteering, you even have a choice to be there. If you are an individual on church staff and you have the privilege of being paid staff, the volunteers should be even more important to you. Exemplifying grace is easier with a plan and a focus. Plan and focus is developed through strategizing the church's yearly event calendar and making a point to understand what is coming in advance to be prepared for. By planning ahead, you are being better prepared and not caught by anything unexpected. This brings more stability to your team and the culture of the church. When stability is added to your team, it builds into that culture a pathway to exemplifying grace to others. It is easier to display grace when you as the leader have less anxiety because of better planning.

What leaders should be:

1.) Intelligent- able to think on their own and problem solve.

2.) Self- Confident (not boastful, but understanding they can handle the job).

3.) Determined to succeed, regardless of the odds.

4.) Have and demonstrate integrity.

5.) Sociability- or the ability to be tactful and interact in a positive way with others.

Leaders' role:

1.) Focus and keep volunteers focused on the main thing.

2.) Define vision and focus.

3.) Remove road blocks for the volunteers to be successful.

4.) Mitigate risks for the team and volunteers.

5.) Communicate effectively.

Function roles, what leaders should be, and what leaders do, are the three components of a successful leader. All wrapped up into one main component, leaders are called to do all of that while demonstrating grace to those that are within their teams. Demonstrating grace is certainly harder than it sounds, but consider this: when you do something that you consider valuable, and you give your own time without immediate compensation, you want to know that your work is appreciated. From a volunteer's perspective, the only way that this is demonstrated is by a leader being gracious. A leader being gracious adds value to the engagement and interaction and gives the individuals volunteering purpose and focus. Ephesians 2:8-9 explains that as we have experienced the value of God's grace, first-hand in our own lives, we should demonstrate it to others in the same way. The key to unlock the door of grace is to be empathetic.

As we serve, in the capacity as leaders, we have to embrace the ideology that it is not about us. The leadership model that we choose to apply to our ministry team speaks volumes about us. The most effective model for church teams is servant leadership. Servant leadership starts in your heart, with you answering the question- "who are you as a human being?". Followed up by the questions: "Are you here to serve or be served?". Your role in life, as it impacts others, determines your success as a ministry team leader. What the motives of your heart are, speaks volumes about who

> ~ Servant leadership is an effective model for ministry teams. ~

you are as a person and where your ego lies. There are two types of ego problems. The first ego problem is false pride. False pride assumes that you know more than any other person, and you are better than they are. It also assumes that your knowledge of the subject matter is more impactful than anyone else's, and that you are the most valuable to your team. The challenge with this ego problem is that it is distracting and takes our focus off of the success of the team. The second type of ego problem is fear and self-doubt. As a leader you are focused on your own personal inadequacies, to the point of

> ~ A leader's responsibility is to help volunteers be successful. ~

team failure, because your focus is not on helping others succeed or the overall mission. Both types of ego problems we see regularly in church ministry teams, and in many cases in safety and security ministries within the church. If you are wanting a successful ministry team, then the culture of the team needs to be absent of ego problems. Leadership culture can only be accomplished with completely engaged volunteers. Your job as a leader is to help your people be successful. Make a difference for and with your people. Build value and equity into your relationships by performing and performing well. Self-worth comes from Christ and the value that He has placed on us. The value that He placed on us, begins with an understanding of His purpose and mission on Earth. The self-worth of others is demonstrated through us actively applying grace to our teams. Grace is combining all of these aspects and understanding that how we interact with others, regardless if they are right or wrong, impacts how they are motivated and if we are successful or not. They might listen to you because you are the leader, but as a volunteer, if they are not sensing respect and value from you (in the form of you as the leader being gracious) they will quickly leave from the team. Being kind and empathetic to others, while remaining flexible is the best way to demonstrate the love of God and exemplify grace to everyone that is on your team.

FOR WHEREVER THERE IS JEALOUSY AND SELFISH AMBITION, THERE YOU WILL FIND DISORDER AND EVIL OF EVERY KIND.

JAMES 3:16

CONCLUSION

If you read our Ministry Lifecycle books, on the six-step process to have a successful ministry, then you know one of the steps is to *Engage* with our volunteers. Our volunteers need to be trained, equipped, engaged, and follow an active framework to be motivated. Being motivated accomplishes the mission or tasks at hand. A final thought on this, is that as leaders we are responsible for managing their performance. We need to be planning (telling them expectations), coaching (advising them how to get there), and evaluating (showing them how to do it successfully). Helping them win at their activities builds unity within the team, but it helps everyone win, not just the leader. When ministry teams only focus on tasks and not volunteer engagement, the culture of the team is not established and will eventually fall apart. As a leader, how do you want to be remembered? What are you core values that you are interested in impressing upon others to be successful? Creating a servant leadership culture allows us to: create a vision, offer clear values, and establish clear internal goals. Doing this creates a culture and ministry where people care about what is happening and how they can impact and support the mission in a positive way with a positive outcome.

A successful leader is one that is prepared. They know what they want to accomplish and the end result that is desired. They know if their goals are reasonable and they know how to communicate those goals to volunteers on their team making everyone successful. It is not learned over night. But it can be learned and it can allow the ministry team to be very successful.

As a leader are you:

1.) Proactive (knowing how to be prepared beforehand for whatever may come).

2.) Reactive (only able to respond and address an incident after it has taken place).

The placement of your values and culture on being proactive or reactive can make or break your ministry team. If your team is involved with church safety and security, being proactive or reactive can have devastating effects on the success of your team. As leaders we need to be proactive for what might be coming ahead, and take the time to invest in those around us, while planning out the future. Then, and only then can we be successful and make our ministry team successful to accomplish the mission of the church. When we are reactive, often times that demonstrates to our team that we have not adequately planned and this "knee jerk" reaction ends up eroding the successful culture of the team.

For More Information on Leading Your Ministry Team:

The Ministry Lifecycle is available to learn about in the book:

Inspire, Influence, Impact

Church Safety & Security Ministry

INSPIRE
INFLUENCE
IMPACT

Embracing the Ministry Lifecycle™
to Take Your
Team Beyond Sunday Mornings

James P. McGarvey
Michael C. Scully

God's Plan for Salvation:

You are not reading this by accident. God loves you. He wants you to have a personal relationship with Him through Jesus, His Son. There is just one thing that separates you from God. That one thing is sin.

People tend to divide themselves into groups - good people and bad people. But God says that every person who has ever lived is a sinner, and that any sin separates us from God. No matter how we might classify ourselves, this includes you and me. We are all sinners.

"For all have sinned and come short of the glory of God."
Romans 3:23

God DOES love you! More than you can ever imagine! And there is nothing you can do to make Him stop! Yes, our sins demand punishment - the punishment of death and separation from God. But, because of His great love, God sent His only Son Jesus to die for our sins.

"God demonstrates His own love for us in this: While we were still sinners, Christ died for us." Romans 5:8

You cannot make yourself right with God by being a better person. Only God can rescue us from our sins.

He is willing to do this not because of anything you can offer Him, but JUST BECAUSE HE LOVES YOU!

> *"He saved us, not because of righteous things we had done, but because of His mercy." Titus 3:5*

It is God's grace that allows you to come to Him - not your efforts to "clean up your life" or work your way to Heaven. You cannot earn it. It is a free gift.

> *"For it is by grace you have been saved, through faith - and this not from yourselves, it is the gift of God - not by works, so that no one can boast." Ephesians 2:8-9*

For you to come to God, the penalty for your sin must be paid. God's gift to you is His son, Jesus, who paid the debt for you when He died on the Cross.

> *"For the wages of sin is death, but the gift of God is eternal life in Jesus Christ our Lord." Romans 6:23*

Jesus paid the price for your sin and mine by giving His life on a cross at a place called Calvary, just outside of the city walls of Jerusalem in ancient Israel. God brought Jesus back from the dead. He provided the way for you to have a personal relationship with Him through Jesus. When we realize how deeply our sin grieves the heart of God and how desperately we need a Savior, we are ready to receive God's offer of salvation. To admit we are sinners means turning away from our sin and selfishness and turning to follow Jesus. The Bible word for this is "repentance" - to change our thinking about how grievous sin is, so our thinking is in line with God's.

All that is left for you to do is to accept the gift that Jesus is holding out for you right now.

> *"If you confess with your mouth, "Jesus is Lord," and believe in your heart that God raised him from the dead, you will be saved. For it is with your heart that you believe and are justified, and it is with your mouth that you confess and are saved." Romans 10:9-10*

God says that if you believe in His Son, Jesus, you can live forever with Him in heaven and He will give you daily guidance in living your life.

> *"For God so loved the world that He gave his one and only Son, that whoever believes in him shall not perish, but have eternal life." John 3:16*

Are you ready to accept the gift of eternal life that Jesus is offering you right now?

Here is a Suggested Prayer:

"Lord Jesus, I know I am a sinner and I do not deserve eternal life and a relationship with You. But I believe that You died and rose from the grave to give me eternal life, and to have a relationship with me, because You love me. Jesus, come into my life, take control of my life, forgive my sins and save me. I am now placing my trust in You alone for my salvation and accept Your gift of forgiveness and eternal life. Amen."

If you have prayed that prayer, welcome to God's family! We would love to hear about it and rejoice with you, as well as talk to you about the "next steps". Reach out to us and let us know!

Ways to Contact Us: church_safety_guy@outlook.com

Website: www.churchsafetyguys.com

ABOUT THE AUTHOR

James P. McGarvey, Ph.D., CPS

James is a best-selling author, public speaker, broadcast host and church security expert. He has served in Central Ohio as Safety Director of a mid-size church for over 15 years. He has over 30 years' experience in Public Safety working as an EMT, Firefighter, EMS Dispatcher, Disaster Chaplain, in Executive Protection and Volunteer officer for the San Bernardino County Sheriff's Office.

James has served in church operations, all over the United States, for the last 30 years as associate pastor, youth pastor and many other leadership roles. He is an educator and curriculum designer in leadership, logistics and business. Presently he works in logistics for the U.S. Defense Department. He regularly coaches churches all over the United States in best practices for safety and security.

BRAND-NEW RESOURCE:
THE CHURCH SECURITY APP!

Available today on the IOS or Android Stores!

Scan this

QR code to

Download!

TO PROTECT AND SERVE

WAR READY

THE ROAD LESS TRAVELED

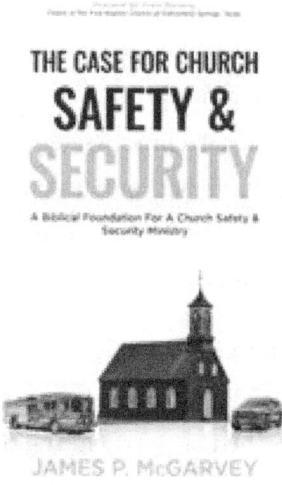

THE CASE FOR CHURCH SAFETY & SECURITY

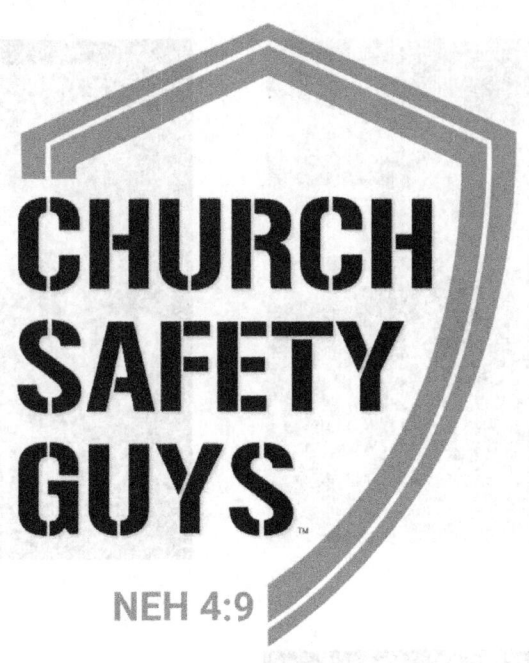

CHURCH
SAFETY
GUYS

NEH 4:9

We are a nonprofit ministry. Our mission is to inspire, influence and impact church safety & security teams. We do this through regular interaction with churches in an effort to help them mitigate safety and security concern, engage their teams and disciple their volunteers. Contact us for more information or resources!

For more information or to schedule a speaking engagement, with James McGarvey or one of the other Church Safety Guys, they can be reached at www.churchsafetyguys.com

Made in the USA
Middletown, DE
16 November 2025

21578391R10040